# MY VERY OWN SIMCHAT TORAH BOOK

by
Judyth Robbins Saypol
Madeline Wikler

KAR-BEN COPIES, INC. ROCKVILLE, MARYLAND

# INTRODUCTION

Waving a flag in a Simchat Torah parade, munching candy apples, and being called to the bimah for an aliyah are the memorable experiences from which Jewish identity is made.

The joyousness of the Simchat Torah celebration also has captured the imagination of Soviet Jews who have chosen this day to declare their identity.

Our book focuses on two themes: Torah and renewal.

We introduce Torah in its many connotations—Torah as book, Torah as scroll, Torah as teaching, Torah as Jewish history and tradition, and Torah as weekly synagogue reading.

The Simchat Torah theme of renewal—ending and beginning—ties in well with the endings and beginnings we have marked in the observance of Rosh Hashanah, Yom Kippur, and Sukkot. The cycle of the year, the cycle of the seasons of nature, the cycle of the week culminating in Shabbat, all provide food for thought for classroom and family discussion.

*J.R.S.*
*M.W.*


ISBN 0-930494-11-3.
Published by KAR-BEN COPIES, Inc.
1-800-4-KARBEN
Printed in the United States of America.

# CONTENTS

Some holidays celebrate nature.
Other holidays remind us of important events.
Still other holidays praise great heroes.
Simchat Torah is different.
It is a holiday in honor of a book.
The greatest book of all.
The Torah.

On Simchat Torah we finish reading the Torah and begin it all over again.

# WHAT IS TORAH?

The Torah is five books in one. We call them the Five Books of Moses to remind us that Moses received the Torah on Mount Sinai.

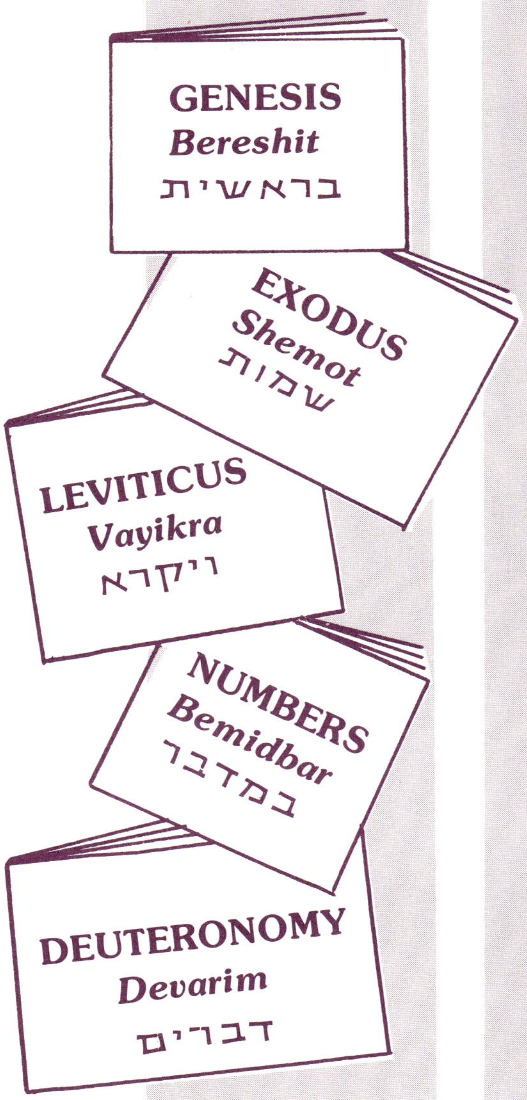


How the world was created.

How the Jewish people began.

Stories of our first fathers and mothers—Abraham, Isaac, and Jacob; Sarah, Rebecca, Rachel, and Leah.

Our freedom from slavery in Egypt.

Moses receiving the Ten Commandments.

Rules for living together in peace and kindness.

Laws to protect the weak, the poor, and the young.

Customs for celebrating holidays and festivals.

How we reached the promised land of Israel.

## READING THE TORAH

Torah means teaching.

The Torah teaches through stories, songs, and poems.

When we gather in the synagogue on Shabbat and holidays, we read from the Torah.

Our rabbis and teachers help us understand how the teachings of the Torah are important today.

The Torah is divided into sections, and we read one each week. It takes exactly one year to read the whole Torah. Each Simchat Torah, we reach the end, and then we start all over from the beginning.

There is never an end to learning.

Each time we read the Torah, we find something new.

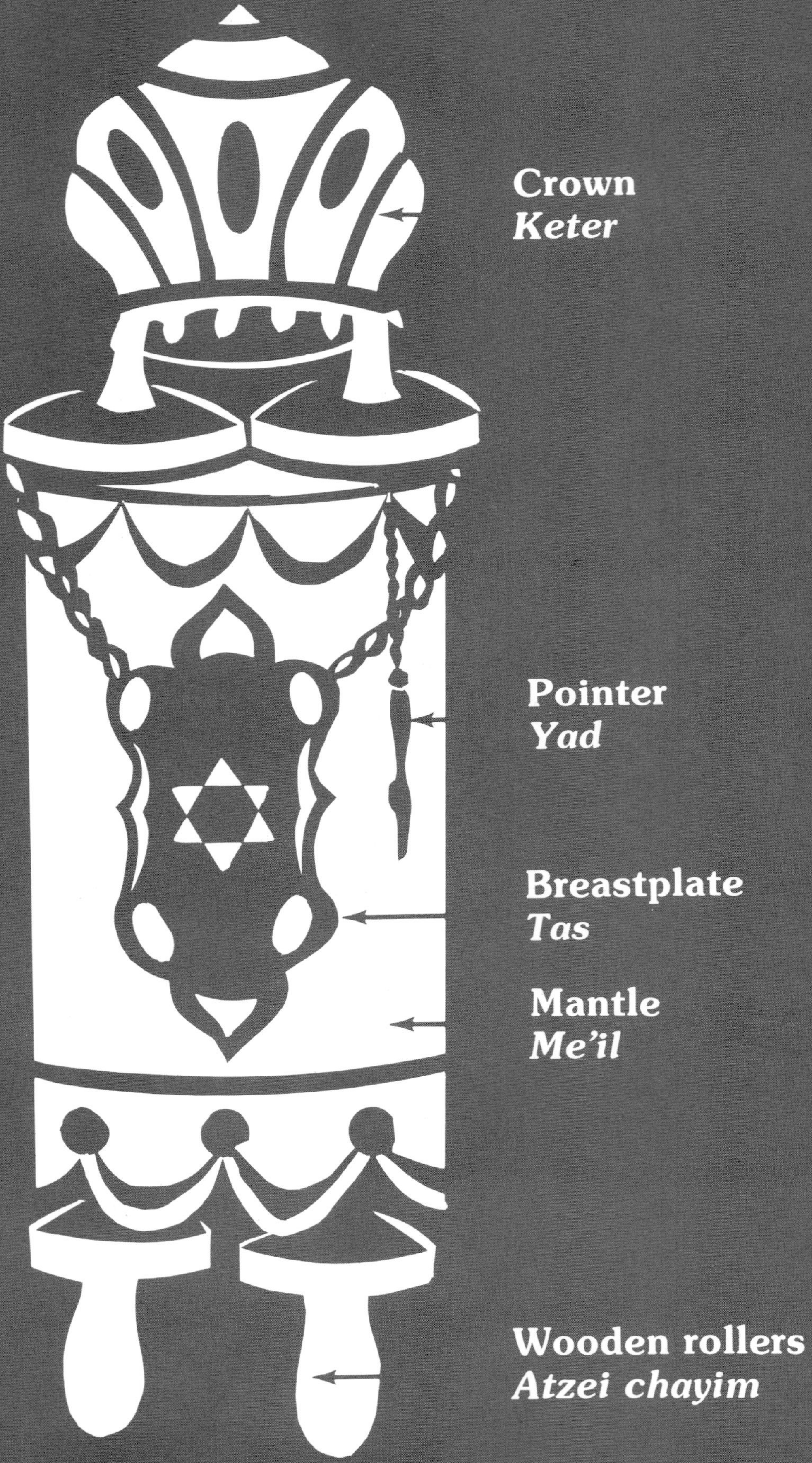
Crown
Keter
Pointer
Yad
Breastplate
Tas
Mantle
Me'il
Wooden rollers
Atzei chayim

## THE TORAH SCROLL

The words of the Torah are written in books. They also are written on the scrolls kept in the ark of every synagogue.

The words of the Torah are copied by a *sofer* or scribe onto large sheets of parchment. The sofer writes with a quill pen, using ink made from the bark of trees. The sheets of parchment are sewn together and tied to wooden rollers to make a scroll.

To honor the Torah, we wrap it in velvet and satin and decorate it with silver and jewels. It is housed in a beautiful ark.

When we read the Torah, we follow the words with a pointer, so that our hands do not touch the scroll.

## SIMCHAT TORAH EVE

Simchat Torah eve is a time of joy and merry-making.

All the Torah scrolls are taken from the ark and paraded around the synagogue seven times.

The parades are called *hakafot.*

Children follow along carrying miniature Torah scrolls and flags of all colors and designs.

The tiniest children ride on the shoulders of the tallest.

The hakafot wind in and out of the aisles, around the bimah, and even out into the street.

People sing and dance with the Torah and each other late into the night.

The honor of being called upon to the bimah to recite the Torah blessings is called *aliyah* which means "to go up."

The rabbi or cantor calls the person by his or her Hebrew name. Each person called for an aliyah recites two blessings—one before and one after the Torah verses are read.

On Shabbat and holidays, only a few people are chosen for an aliyah. On Simchat Torah, everyone has an aliyah—even young children. It is the only time children under the age of Bar and Bat Mitzvah are given this honor. The children gather at the bimah, and a large tallit is spread over them. A beloved member of the congregation recites the blessings a few words at a time, and the children repeat them.

## SIMCHAT TORAH MORNING

On Simchat Torah morning, there are more hakafot, but this time the parades are shorter, because there is much to do. We must finish reading the Torah—and begin it again.

A first scroll is unrolled to the last chapter of the book of *Devarim*. The roller to the right of the reader is very fat, because the whole Torah is on that roller. We have reached the very end.

The last chapters are read many, many times, so that everyone in the congregation can be honored with an aliyah.

The person chosen for the very last aliyah is called the *Chatan Torah*, the bridegroom of the Torah. Simchat Torah is as happy as a wedding.

As the final words are read, the congregation rises and proclaims:

**CHAZAK, CHAZAK**
**VENITCHAZEK**
***May our strength increase!***

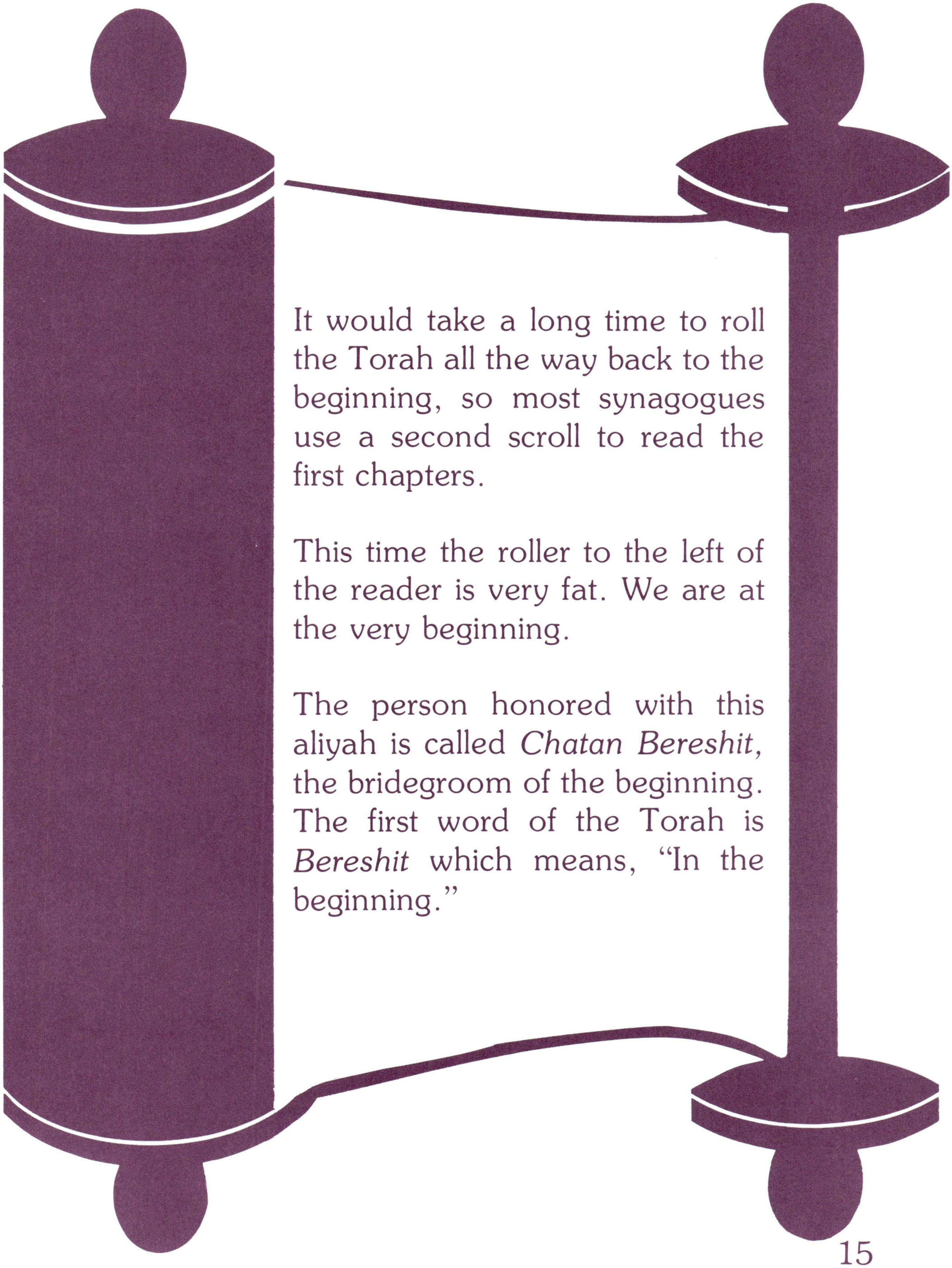

It would take a long time to roll the Torah all the way back to the beginning, so most synagogues use a second scroll to read the first chapters.

This time the roller to the left of the reader is very fat. We are at the very beginning.

The person honored with this aliyah is called *Chatan Bereshit*, the bridegroom of the beginning. The first word of the Torah is *Bereshit* which means, "In the beginning."

## CLOSING TORAH PORTION

### *This is the Blessing*

***Before his death, Moses blessed each of the tribes of the children of Israel.***

***When he finished, Moses climbed Mount Pisgah. God showed him the promised land of Israel.***

***"You may see the land, but you will not live to go there," God said.***

***Moses died and was buried. He was 120 years old.***

***Joshua became the new leader of the Jewish people.***

***There has never been a greater prophet in all Israel than Moses.***

**Devarim**
**Deuteronomy**
**Chapters 33-34**

# BEGINNING TORAH PORTION

## *In the Beginning*

*In the beginning, God created the heavens and earth,*

*The land and the seas and the sky,*

*The sun and the moon and the stars,*

*The trees and the flowers,*

*The birds and the fish,*

*The animals and people.*

*When God was finished creating the world,*

*God created a day for rest.*

*God called it Shabbat.*

**Bereshit**
**Genesis**
**Chapters 1-2**

When the Torah reading is over, merrymaking begins. In some synagogues, members of the congregation take turns being the rabbi and cantor. Their sermons and chanting are lots of fun. The afternoon ends with singing, dancing, and snacks for all.

## CONSECRATION

Simchat Torah celebrates learning. Because it comes at the beginning of the school year, it is the holiday some synagogues choose to honor their new students.

The congregation may have a Consecration Service. The youngest children march to the bimah and stand before the ark. The rabbi blesses them, and welcomes them to religious school.

Some schools present their new students with a gift of a prayer book or Bible. It is also traditional for the children to receive a sweet treat, so learning may be sweet.

## SOVIET JEWS

For many years, Jews in the Soviet Union were not allowed to read Torah or to learn about Jewish life. The government hoped they would forget they were Jewish.

But they remembered. On Simchat Torah, in Moscow, Riga, Leningrad, and other Soviet cities, Jews would gather at the few remaining synagogues to sing and dance to Hebrew and Yiddish melodies.

Today, Soviet Jews are permitted to celebrate Jewish holidays and attend Hebrew schools. But Simchat Torah is still a special time. Now they gather to celebrate religious freedom, and Jews around the world rejoice with them.

## ENDING AND BEGINNING

As the sun sets on Simchat Torah day, a month of holidays which began with Rosh Hashanah is over.

We have celebrated new beginnings—
a new year,
a new harvest,
a new reading of the Torah.
We have read the story of creation.

But the creation of the world is not finished.
It goes on every day.
Each day we help to create the world:
at work,
at play,
at school.

Shabbat is also a new beginning.
We rest from our work, we celebrate with our families, we learn from the Torah.

For the Jewish people, creation and Torah have no end.

# TORAH BLESSINGS

*Before reading the Torah:*

Thank you, God, for choosing us to receive the gift of Torah.

*After reading the Torah:*

Thank you, God, for the Torah of truth and life everlasting.

# DUNDAI

Folk

Israel without Torah is like a body without a soul.

# SISU V'SIMCHU I

Verse: B. Kaspi

Be happy on this joyous holiday. Clap hands, sing out, join together in praise of God and Israel.

# SISU V'SIMCHU II

Folk

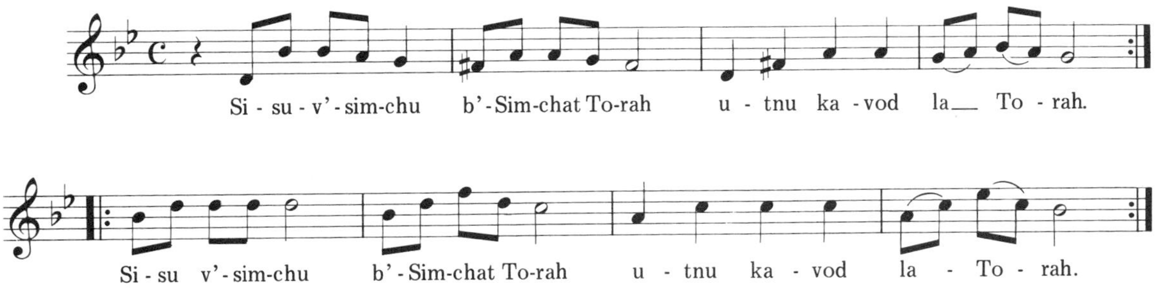


Rejoice and honor the Torah on Simchat Torah.

# TORAH TZIVAH LANU MOSHE

Traditional

*May be sung as a 3-part round.*

The Torah given by Moses is an inheritance of the people Israel.

# BARUCH ELOHENU

Chasidic Melody

2. Venatan lanu Torat emet.
3. Vechaye olam nata b'tochenu.
Blessed be God who created us and gave us the Torah of truth and life everlasting.